Unicorn rainbow Makes

By L.T. Marshall

Welcome to my Knitting Designs.

By L.T. Marshall

● - - - ● - - - ● - - - ● - - - ● - - - ● - - - ● - - - ●

I have been creating knitting patterns for many years for my own benefit and finally decided to write them down for sale. I occasionally share free patterns on my website.

I would say they're suitable for someone with intermediate skill, although a beginner may be able to do just as well with a little more time and patience.

Have fun creating these collectible characters for your family and friends. You can find my creations online under the name One Creative family (formerly Liana Marcel)) or as the author by the name L.T.Marshall. I have a YouTube channel under my new brand - One Creative Family (OCF)

WWW.LTMarshall.Blog

● - - - ● - - - ● - - - ● - - - ● - - - ● - - - ● - - - ●

Contents

Welcome to my Knitting Designs.

By L.T. Marshall

Safety guidelines

The items in these patterns are not suitable for babies and very young children due to small parts , such as buttons and toy eyes.

Knitting yarns

Small oddments of Double knitting in various colours, as stated in the instructions

Abbreviations

P - Purl. P1 - Purl one. Pwise - Purl Wise.
K - Knit. K1 - Knit one. Kwise - Knit Wise
Sts - stitches,
K2 tog - Knit 2 Together. P2 tog - Purl 2 Together.
Inc1 - Increase 1 stitch(Work into front and back of stitch).
Y.Fwd - Yarn forward around needle. St-st - Stocking Stitch.
G-st - Garter stitch, Slp1 - slip one stitch to the other needle without working.

B+T tightly - Break off yarn leaving a long end and thread it through stitches left on knitting needle, pull together tightly then fasten off.

Additional instructions - for some of the detailing you will need to be able to make a chain stitch.

Needles (unless additional sizes stated)

UK sized 10 and 12 - USA sized 3.25mm and 2.5mm

Sparkle The Unicorn

For This Project - You need.

Knitting yarns.

DK wool in
Cream, Pale Lemon and Medium lemon
Hair can be done in rainbow wool as pictured or in separate colours of
your choice.
Silver for horn

Additional materials.

Toy eyes (4mm)
2 seed beads for nose (any size works as long as it's under 3mm)
2 yellow buttons for dungarees (we used micro buttons)

Tools.

I use UK size 10 knitting needles for the unicorn and shorts.
No.12 for the horn
Stuffing
Wool needle.
Sewing needle.
Scissors.

Sparkle The Unicorn

The body and head. (One piece)

Cast on 5 sts in Cream
KW Incl into every st (10sts)
KW Incl into every st (20sts)
(P1, Incl) to end (30sts)
St st 6 rows
(K4, K2tog) to end
P1 row
(K3, K2tog) to end
P2tog, P to last 2 sts, P2tog
Stst 2 rows
**K2tog, K to last 2 sts, K2tog
P1 row ***
Repeat from ** to *** until 14sts remain
Stst 2 rows
Start shaping head here, so mark ends both ends of this row with wool so you know where to gather for neck.
K2, (Incl, K1) to last 2 sts, K2
P1 row
Repeat last 2 rows once more.
Stst 10 rows
(K3, K2tog) to last 2 sts, K2
P1 row
(K2, K2tog) to end
P 1 row
(K1, K2tog) to end
(P2tog) to end
B&T

To make up

From gathered top sew down seams, stuffing as you go until you get to the base. Close base up fully.
Around neck stitch in and out with wool and pull to gather and define neck. Fasten off. Remove your marker wool. If you are using toy eyes, make sure to secure them in place before sewing and stuffing head.

3

Sparkle The Unicorn

The muzzle

Cast on 15sts in Grey
K2, (K1, Inc1) to last 3 sts, K3 (20sts)
Stst 3 rows
(K2, K2tog) to end
(P1, P2tog) to end
(K2tog) to end
B&T

To Make up

Draw tight and sew from gathered top to the cast on edge. Stuff very lightly and sew to Unicorns face as pictured. Sew seed beads in place as nostrils.

Ears (Make 2)

Cast on 8sts in Cream
KW Inc1 in every st (16sts)
P2tog, P to last 2 sts, P2tog
K2tog, K to last 2 sts, K 2tog
P1 row
(K1, K2tog) to end
(P2tog) to end
B&T

To Make up

From B&T end, sew up seams to cast on base. Put the seam to the center back and flatten ear. Sew base shut then gather base to make a more defined ear shape. Sew to unicorns head as pictured.

Legs (Make 2)

Start with Grey
Cast on 4sts
KW Inc1 into every st -8sts
K 1 row
(K1, Inc1) to end - 12sts
K1 row
(K3, Inc1) to end - 15sts
K 1 row
(K4, Inc1) to end - 18sts
K 4 rows
Join on Cream and work as follows
K 1 row
(P5, P2tog) to last 4 sts, P4 - 16sts
K 1 row
(P4 P2tog) to last 4 sts, P4 - 14sts
K1 row
P1, P2tog,P1, P2tog, P2, P2tog, P1, P2tog, P1
K 1 row
Stst 25 rows
(K2tog) to end
B&T

To Make up

Gather grey hoof and then sew seam down to cast on edge. Stuff leg. Close
end and sew in place as pictured on Unicorns body.

Arms (Make 2)

Cast on 3sts
KW Incl into every st - 6sts
K 1 row
(K1, Incl) to end - 9sts
K 1 row
(K3, Incl) to last 1 st, K1 - 11sts
K1 row
(K4, Incl) to end - 13sts
St st 3 rows
Join on Cream and continue as follows
K 1 row
(P5,P2tog)P5) - 13sts
K 1 row
(P4, P2tog) to end - 10 sts
K 1 row
(P3, P2tog) to end - 8sts
K 1 row
Stst 15 rows
(K2tog) to end
B&T

To make Up

Gather grey hoof and then sew seam down to cast on edge. Stuff arm.
Close end and sew in place as pictured on Unicorns body.

Sparkle The Unicorn

Horn

With no. 12 needles and silver
Cast on 6sts
P 1 row
K 1 row
P 1 row
(K2tog) to end
P 1 row
(K2tog) to end
B&T

To Make up

From B&T end, gather tight, stitch sides together to cast on edge. Stuff with a very small amount and sew in place to unicorns face as pictured.

Hair and Tail

Both are done the same way on No.10 needles.
For Hair you will cast on 20sts, and cast off again. this makes one strand of hair.
You will need 14 strands this length. 1 strand 15sts, 1 strand 10sts, for the mane.
The tail is made of 7 strands of 30sts

To Make up

For the mane I knitted my strands in pairs. one pair was one colour, so I used 7 colours. Each pair was on colour. I then sewed them across the back of the head. Layering the next pair directly above.
I did this with the 20sts strands until i got to the top of the head, then the 15st strand and then the 10st strand to make a fringe. The horn is sewn in front of that.

The Tail strands are all sewn together at the base to make a 'ponytail' and sewn to the unicorns rump.

At this point Sparkle is complete and you can blush his cheeks with pink sharpie marker to add some life into his face.

7

Dungaree shorts

The shorts

Starting with one leg
No.10 needles and dark Lemon
Cast on 20sts
K 2 rows
Join Light Lemon
St 2 rows starting P
You will work in stripes of 2 rows per colour, each.
St St 2 rows Dark
St St 2 rows light
Leave this leg on a spare needle and make a 2nd the exact same way.

Put both legs on needles with wrong sides facing
P across both legs in Dark
St st 4 rows(Continue stripe pattern)
(K2, K2tog) to end
P 1 row
(K4, K2tog) to end
St st 4 rows
Gst 2 rows in Dark
Cast off.

To Make up

Sew the legs closed by folding the side seam into the center and sewing under the crotch. Close both legs and slide on the unicorn to see how far you should sew up before you meet the tail. Stop stitching here. Over the seams left open to neaten.

Dungaree shorts

The Straps (Make 2)

In Dark Lemons and no.10 needles.
Cast on 20sts
Cast off.

To Make up

Straighten out by stretching very lightly. Sew one end to the back of the shorts where you left it open, Then cross across the unicorns back and bring strap over front to be sewn as pictured. Do same for other strap on other side.
The cross offer design means the trousers need no closure on the back to accommodate the tail and the shorts are removable.
Sew buttons on the front as pictured to finish.
You are done.

Outfit for Sparkle The Unicorn

For This Project - You need.

Knitting yarns.

DK in Light aqua
Dark Aqua

Additional materials.

2 buttons for detail

Tools.

I use size 10 knitting needles for the dress and bag
No.12 for the flower
Wool needle.
Sewing needle.
Scissors.

Outfit for Sparkle The Unicorn

Dress

Cast on 40sts in Light aqua
P 1 row
K1, (Yfwd, K2tog through back of sts, K1, K2tog, Yfwd, K1).... repeat until 2 sts remain, K2
P 1 row
K2, (Yfwd, slp1, K2tog, Pass slipped stitch over the knit st, yfd, k3) Repeat to last 2 sts, K2
Stst 8 rows
(K2, K2tog) to end
P 1 row
(K4, K2tog) to end
Stst 5 rows

Join on dark aqua
K2 rows
P1 row
K 1 row
Rejoin light aqua
K 1 row
Stst 3 rows

Separating the bodice
K6, turn
P2tog, p4
Stst 4 rows on these 5 sts only.
Cast off

Rejoin to rest of sts on needle.
K13, turn
P2tog, P9, P2tog
Stst 4 rows on these 11 sts only
Cast off.

Rejoin to last 6 sts
K6
P4, P2tog
Stst 4 rows
Cast off

Outfit for Sparkle The Unicorn

To Make Up

Sew from base of skirt up an inch, bring side seams together, fasten off here.
This will sit below sparkles tail.
Over sew edges of the rest of the two sides. On one side you will apply a
button just above sparkles tail, and one at the neckline.
To make buttonholes on the opposite side chain 5sts on matching wool and
sew loops at the same levels as the buttons.
For the dress straps, you join the back pieces to the front at the armholes by
chaining a 5st chain between the two pieces to make a suitable arm hole and
strappy straps.

Flower

In dark aqua
Cast on 21sts on No.12 needles
Cast on 4sts
Sl1, K2, turn
P2, turn
K3, turn
P2tog twice.
Repeat all of these rows 4 more times.
B+T

To Make up

When you gather the B+T it will pull the flower into shape and bring the
petals together, Sew the seam halfway to join the open edge. Sew in place on
the dress and put a button in the center.

Outfit for Sparkle The Unicorn

Bag

Cast on 20sts in dark aqua
P1 row
(K2, Incl) to last 2 sts, K2
Stst 8 rows
P2, P2tog, Cast off, 5, P2tog, P5, P2tog, Cast off 5, P2tog, P1
K3, turn
Cast off
Rejoin to next set of sts
K7, turn
Cast off
Rejoin to last sts
K3, Turn
Cast off.

Straps (Make 2)

Cast on 15sts
Cast off

Bag Closure

Cast on 5 sts
Cast off

To Make up

Join bag side seams and sew up, move to center back before sewing the base shut. The straps are attached at either side of the dip in the bag on each side of the bag. The closure is sewn above the back seam of the bag. To make a button loop, chain 5sts on the end of the other side. Sew a button in center of bag to close the bag.

13

Star Rainbow Doll

For This Project - You need.

Knitting yarns.

Chosen flesh colour 50g
White 50g
Brown 50g
Small 50g balls in Red, Orange, Yellow, Green, Blue, Purple, Pink
Navy 50g

Additional materials.

Embroidery thread in black and pink
Optional seed beads for eyes
Sharpie to blush cheeks in pale pink
Toy Stuffing – Small bag.
Micro button for the bag

Tools.

No.10 needles UK sized
No. 5 needles UK (5.5mm USA) for underskirts
Wool needle.
Sewing needle.
Scissors.

Star Rainbow Doll

Head and Body

Right Leg

On No.10 needles and in yellow cast on 10sts
Inc Kwise into every St - 20 sts
Start with K row
St St 6 rows
K1, (k3tog) 4 times, K7 - 12 sts
P1 row
Add red to start the stripe pattern.
In the following order St St 2 rows of each colour
Red, Orange, Yellow, Green, Blue, Purple Pink
Repeat the stripe pattern one more time for each colour.
Put on a spare needle to make the second leg.

Left Leg

On No.10 needles and in yellow cast on 10sts
Inc Kwise into every St - 20 sts
Start with K row
St St 6 rows
K7, (k3tog) 4 times, K1 - 12 sts
P1 row
Add red to start the stripe pattern.
In the following order St St 2 rows of each colour
Red, Orange, Yellow, Green, Blue, Purple Pink
Repeat the stripe pattern one more time for each colour.
Bring back two legs to one needle and in Navy K across both sets of stitches to join them.
24 sts.

The Body

Starting with P row
St St 16 rows
Add yellow and K2 rows to create a dress edge

Star Rainbow Doll

.
Add flesh colour
K 1 row to bring work back to order
St St 3 rows
(K2tog) to end
P1 row
Kwise into every st for head
St St 10 rows
(K2tog) to end
(P2tog) to end
B+T

To Make Up

Start at head, and sew down to where the legs join on. Stuff head and body
and close between legs.
Sew down each leg, stuffing as you go and end at the feet, sewing foor
closed in a straight line from toe to heel on the base.
Draw a length of wool around neck using an in out stitch and draw tight to
define neck.

Skirt

Top Layer

In Dark blue/Navy and size 10 needles
Cast on 75sts
St St 12 rows
(K3tog) to end
Cast off Pwise

Middle Layer

With no.5 needles and white
(If you have no large needles you can make the skirts on whatever larger
size you have or repeat top layer skirt 3 times for the layers instead.)
Cast on 50sts
Working in K only rows (Gst)
Gst 7 rows

16

(K2tog) to end
Cast off

Bottom Layer

Cast on 40 sts on size 5 needles in white
Gst 5 rows
(K2tog) to end
Cast off

To Make up

Join the skirt pieces at the edges to create 3 skirts. On the doll locate the middle of the torso and mark for the navy skirt piece. Below this you want to sew on first the under layer, then middle and sew the navy one on top to create the puffy skirt.

If the white middle skirt is too large on the waist then gather slightly while sewing in place.

The navy layer will curl at the edges but you can iron or wet pin this out before applying if you like. I left mine to curl and expose the under layer.

The belt

In red and no 10 needles
Cast on 28sts
Cast off.

Sew belt around waist to hide where skirt joins and secure ends at the middle back.

Star Rainbow Doll

Arms (make 2)

Size 10 needles and Navy
Cast on 10sts
St st 6 rows
Attach yellow
K2 rows
Attach flesh
Start with a K row
St st 10 rows
(K1, Kwise) to end to create hands
St st 4 rows
(p2tog) to end
(k2tog) to end
B+T

To Make Up

Sew from hands to open cast on edge, stuff and sew the arms closed by flattening the top so the seam lies at the center back, Sew across top of arm in a straight line and leave aside for sleeve frills.

Navy Sleeve Frill

With No.10 needles and Navy
Cast on 20sts
St St 4 rows
(K2tog) to last st
Cast off Pwise

White Sleeve Frill

With no.10 needles and white
Cast on 15sts
St st 3 rows
(K2tog) to last st, K1
Cast off Pwise

Star Rainbow Doll

To Make Up

Sew the sleeve frill cast off edge to top of arm. Sew edges down the sides around the half way mark on each arm to create a cap sleeve. The navy frill is sewn right over the top of this to create a half sleeve effect. (Pictures show how it should be)
Then the arm is sewn in place on the doll at the top of the shoulder and a few stitches down each side to hold the arm in a downward position.

Boot ankle trim (make 2)

In yellow and No 10 needles
Cast on 14sts
Cast off
Join at center back of ankle and stitch in place just above boot to tidy that area

Bag

In light blue and no 10 needles
Cast on 8sts
St st 15 rows
(P2tog) to end
K1 row
(P2tog) to end
B+T

To Make Up

The bag is folded almost in half length ways, leaving a small triangle peeking out the top which is folded over to create the flap. Sew sides and flap down and add button detail to finish.
To make strap finger chain a length that fits around her body and sew to each side of bag.

Star Rainbow Doll

The Hair

Using Brown I cut my wool into 30cm lengths until I had a substantial pile.
Taking 3 strands at a time, I folded them in half and stitched along a hairline around the entire head.
I then stitched a few more in the top centre part area of the dolls head to add volume when all hair was pulled up into a ponytail.
This means your doll has a bare head inside the hairline apart from at the top area to create a full ponytail.
To add volume at the sides I added a second row of hair behind the ear area.
I then pulled all wool into a ponytail and secured with a lnegth of wool wrapped around and stitched through for extra hold.

The hair band

In light blue and no. 10 needles
Cast on 14sts
Cast off
Join at center back of ponytail and stitch in place to tidy that area and hide the wrapped wool.

Star Rainbow Doll

The Face

I used embroidery thread to make my smile and eyes in black if you have no beads. (seed beads were used on the doll as eyes)

You can use a pale sharpie marker to blush the cheeks.

And you're done!!

Star's Unicorn

You can knit this in Snuggly DK wool too for a fluffy version.

For This Project - You need.

Knitting yarns.

100g ball of white
100g ball of multicolour
50g ball of lemon

Additional materials.

Black embroidery thread
Pink sharpie marker
Toy Stuffing – medium bag.

Tools.

No.10 needles.
No.8 needles uk (USA 4.0mm)
Wool needle.
Sewing needle.
Scissors.

Star's Unicorn

Front legs, neck and head. (One piece)

Cast on 28 Sts on No.10 needles in Lemon. (this will be the back of the hooves)
St st 6 rows.
Next row - ** K2tog, K to last 2 Sts, K2tog.
P1 row*
Break off Lemon, add white
P1 row
This switches the work to face the opposite way.
Repeat from ** to * until you have 20 Sts, ending with the P row.
St st 20 rows.
Leave this on a needle and make a second leg in the same way.

Put both sets of stitches on one needle (40 Sts) with right side facing, then knit across both legs to join.
St st 15 rows.
Next row -***K2tog, K to last 2 sts , K2tog.
P1 row**.
Repeat from *** to ** until 30 Sts remain, ending with a P row.

Increase for the head as follows.
K5, (Inc 1, K1) to last 5 Sts, K5.
P1 row. (40 Sts)
Repeat last 2 rows once more. (55Sts)
St st 18 rows.
Next row - (K3, K2tog) to end.
P1 row.
Next row - (K2, K2tog) to end .
P1 row.
Next row - (K1, K2tog) to end.
P2 tog to end.
B+T tightly.

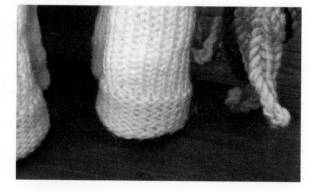

21

To make up

Sew from top of the head, down to where the neck is and stuff. Draw a little wool through the increase for head row and pull tight for neck (using an in and out stitch around the neck and pulling a little tighter to draw in). Sew down body and stuff as you go to the point where legs begin.
Sew legs from joint between legs down each and stuff leaving bases of the feet open. There will be a flat line down back of horses head this is normal and is where the mane will be sewn on.
Leave this piece aside for now.

Star's Unicorn

Back legs and rump.

Leg (Make 2)

Cast on 28 Sts on No.10 needles in lemon.
St st 6 rows.
Next row -**k2tog, k to last 2 sts , k2tog
Next row - P1 row*
Break off Lemon, add white
P1 row
This switches the work to face the opposite way.
Repeat from ** to *, until you have 20 Sts ending with the P row
St st 20 rows
Leave on a spare needle and make 2nd leg in same way

One second piece is knitted put both sets of stitches on one needle (40 sts)
right side facing and knit across both legs
Next row - St st 15 rows
Next row - (p3, p2tog) to end
Next row - K 1 row
Next row - (P1, p2tog) to end
Next row - k 1 row
Next row - (p2tog)to end
B+t tightly

To make up

Draw thread tightly and sew down to where legs meet, stuff well.
Join legs and sew down each one, stuffing and leaving bases open.

Foot base (Make 4)

Cast on 30 Sts on No.10 needles in Lemon.
K1 row.
(K2, K2tog) to last 2 Sts - K2.
K1 row.
(K1, K2 tog) to last 2 Sts - K2.
K1 row.
(K2 tog) to end.
B+T tightly.

23

To make up

Flatten out and sew edges to make a flat circle. Sew this onto horses legs at the base, closing the base up and giving it a flat pad to stand on. Do this with all 4 legs.
I have found the best method is to tuck the base inside the open foot, so the rim sits under the edge of the leg edge. It makes it flatter and easier to sew in place. Also allows some error in size.

Middle section of body

Cast on 15 Sts on No.10 needles in white
St st until work measures 25 cm. (this can vary depending on your knitting tension but ideally you want a piece that sits snugly around the Unicorn center that matches up with your legs on either side.
If you make a piece too long, you can overlap the edges.
Cast off.

To make up

Sew cast off edge to cast on edge, making a tube shape. Stuff lightly to hold shape and sew back legs to one open end and front legs to other - making sure the seams are facing into the tube on both pieces, and the stomach seam faces down. Add more stuffing before closing completely, to stiffen. This is quite tricky to sew together and you may find using safety pins to hold in place while sewing helpful.

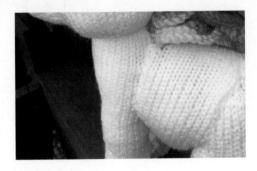

Star's Unicorn

Ears (make 2)

Cast on 20 Sts on No.10 needles in white
K1 row.
Next row - (P4, P2tog) to last 2 Sts, P2.
K1 row.
Next row - (P3, P2tog) to last 2 Sts, P2.
K1 row.
Next row - (P2, P2tog) to last 2 Sts, P2.
K1 row.
Next row - (P1, P2tog) to last 2 sts, P2.
K1 row
Next row - (P2 tog) to end.
K1 row.
B+T tightly.

To make up

Fold in half and flatten to make a triangle shape. Sew up seam, leaving it to one side of the ear and sew onto horses head at each side. Position is optional. Sew in place with seam pointing the center of head.

Star's Unicorn

Muzzle

Cast on 30 Sts on No.10 needles in white
K 1 row.
P2tog, P to last 2 sts, P2 tog.
K 1 row.
Repeat these last 2 rows until 20 Sts remain, ending on K row.
P2tog to end (10 Sts)
K2tog to end (5 Sts)
B+T tightly.

To make up

Draw tightly to close the end, sew up side seam. Stuff lightly and sew onto front of Unicorns face. Leave enough space on the upper part of face for eyes and fringe.

Hair

With No.8 needles and multicoloured wool
Cast on 15 Sts.
Cast off, leaving 1 st remaining on needle, use this stitch to cast on another 15 Sts.
Cast off again, leaving one St remaining on needle.
You will notice this makes the hair strands, yet keeps them joined in a line.
Continue using 30 Sts instead of 15, until you have the 2 short strands and 16 longer ones. Make another 2 with the 15 Sts and cast off the last one completely.

To make up.

You should have a long chain of strands which can be flattened out.
Fold this in half, bringing the short ones together. These are the fringe and get sewn between the ears. Sew remainder down the back of the head along the visible seam in a line.

Star's Unicorn

Tail

The tail is made in exactly the same way, except casting on 40 Sts and continuing for 8 strands before casting off. It is then sewn with all the strands pulled together at top to form a tail and sewn on the rump.

Horn

With No.10 needles, Lemon wool
Cast on 10 Sts
K1 row.
P1 row.
K2tog, K to last 2 Sts, K2tog .
P1 row.
Repeat these last 2 rows until 2 Sts remain.
P2tog
B+T tightly.

To make up

Sew up to cast on edge, stuff and sew onto unicorns face, just below fringe and centered.

To finish.

With black thread using chain stitch outline the eyes and add eyelashes as pictured, Then stitch white highlight in the inner pupil.

Add two french knots on the muzzle for nostrils and chain stitch a curved line below them for the mouth.

I blushed the cheeks using a pale pink sharpie permanent marker lightly over the area.

George the Unicorn.

For This Project - You need.

Knitting yarns.

Cream
Grey
Sunflower yellow
Fuchsia, Purple, Blue, Green, yellow, orange and red for belly or you can
use a variegated rainbow wool

Additional materials.

Embroidery thread in Black or toy eyes
Toy Stuffing – Small bag.
Pink Sharpie to blush cheeks

Tools.

No.10 needles. UK sized
Wool needle. UK sized
Sewing needle.
Scissors.

28

George the Unicorn.

Legs (Make 2)

In sunflower yellow and size 10 needles
Cast on 10sts
Incl into every st (20sts)
P2 rows
Starting with a P row, Stst 4 rows
Join Cream
(P1, P2tog) to last st, P1
Stst 25 rows
(P3tog) to last 2 sts, P2tog
B+T

Body

Starting in Fuschia, cast on 9sts
P 1 row
Incl into every st (18sts)
P 1 row
(K1, Incl) to end
Join purple
P 1 row
(K2, Incl) to end
Stst 2 rows purple
Join blue
Stst 4 rows
Join green
Stst 3 rows
(K4, K2tog) to end
Join Yellow
Stst 4 rows
Join orange
Stst 4 rows
Join red
P 1 row
(K1, K2tog) to end
P 1 row
(K1, Incl) to end
Join Cream
P 1 row

29

George the Unicorn.

(K2, Incl) to end (40sts)
Stst 20 rows
(P2, P2tog) to end
(K1, K2tog) to end
(P2tog) to end
B+T

To make up

Sew from top of the head, down to where the neck is and stuff. Draw a little wool through the increase for head row and pull tight for neck (using an in and out stitch around the neck and pulling a little tighter to draw in). Sew down body and stuff as you go to base, Gather and close.

Legs are sewn down from B+T to yellow hoof, stuffing as you go. Sew base of foot shut. It should have a flat foot base. Sew legs on the bottom of the unicorn as pictured.

30

George the Unicorn.

In Sunflower yellow, cast on 8sts
Incl into every st
P2 rows
Start P, Stst 3 rows
Join Cream
(K1, K2tog) to end
Stst 15 rows
(K2tog) to last st, P1
B+T

To make up

Draw thread tightly and sew down to hoof, stuff well.
Join to body as pictured.

31

George the Unicorn.

Muzzle

Cast on 20 Sts on No.10 needles in Cream
Stst 5 rows
(P2tog) to end
(K2tog) to end
B+T

To make up

Sew down from gathered end to Cast on edge, leaving base open.Stuff and
sew directly to Unicorns face as pictured.

Ears (make 2)

Cast on 15sts in cream
Stst 3 rows
(P1, P2tog) to end
K 1 row
(P1, P2tog) to end
K 1 row
(P2tog) to last st, P1
B+T

To Make Up

Sew down from gathered end to cast on edge, turn seam to middle back
and flatten the piece to form a triangle. Sew base closed flat. Gather ear in
the center to pinch it a little and sew to head as pictured.

George the Unicorn.

Horn

In sunflower yellow
Cast on 8sts
Stst 2 rows
(P1, P2tog) to last 2 sts, P2
K 1 row
(P1, P2tog) to end
K 1 row
(P2tog) twice
B+T

To make up

Sew from gathered end to cast on edge, creating a horn. Stuff very
lightly and sew to face in desired position.

Hair

Cast on 15 Sts in grey.
Cast off, leaving 1 st remaining on needle, use this stitch to cast on another
15 Sts.
Cast off again.
This makes a pair of hair strands,
You will need to make 12 pairs to work up the back of the head

Tail

The tail is made the same as the hair, except you cast on 20sts and do not
cast off fully after 2 strands. Continue using the single stitch to cast on
more until you have 5 strands before fully casting off.

33

George the Unicorn.

To make up

Sew the hair pairs vertically in the center back of the head, one above the other until you work up the head and over until just behind the horn.

The tail is gathered to create a tail base and sewn in place on the rump.

To finish.

If you are using toy eyes, they should have been inserted before the head was sewn shut. You can use embroidery thread for eyes if you prefer. Blush the cheeks with a pink marker, very lightly.

34

Rainbow Hanger

For This Project - You need.

Knitting yarns.

DK wool in
Red, Orange, yellow, Green, Blue, Purple, Pink
White for clouds
Blue for raindrops

Additional materials.

A5 sheet white felt
Scrap card
Toy Stuffing – Small bag.
3 x 8mm beads

Tools.

No.10 needles. UK sized
Wool needle.
Sewing needle.
Scissors.

Rainbow Hanger

Rainbow (make 2)

With Pink and size 10 needles
Cast on 10 sts
(incl) into every St (20sts)

Join Purple
P1 row
K6, Incl, K6, Incl, K6

Join Blue
P1 row
K6, Incl, K4, Incl, K4, Incl, K5

Join Green
P1 row
K6, (Incl, K3) until last 7 sts, K7

Join Yellow
P1 row
K6, (Incl, K2) to last 7 sts, K7

Join Orange
P1 row
K6 (Incl, K1) to last 7 sts, K7

Join Red
P1 row
Cast off

To Make Up

When both pieces are made lay one on card and lightly draw around. Cut
the card out smaller than the rainbow so it sits snugly inside the two pieces
when faced back to back. Use this as a template to cut out two white felt
ones the same. Sandwich the felt on either side of the card to pad the
rainbow when stitched together. The rainbow pieces should be sewn on
with right sides facing out so your rainbow is double sided.

36

Rainbow Hanger

Cloud

With white cast on 10 sts
Inc1 into each st - 20sts
Stst 4 rows
P4, turn
K1 row on these 4 sts
P2tog twice
B&T

Rejoin wool to remaining sts
P 1 row
K4, turn
P2tog twice, turn
B&T these 4 sts

Rejoin wool to sts on needles
K 1 row
P6, turn
K1 row on these 6 sts
P2tog three times
B&T these 6 sts

Rejoin to last 6 sts
P1 row
K 1 row
P2tog, three times
B&T

To Make up

The cloud is folded in half between the two middle clouds. Use the threads to over sew the edges to neaten them up and sew around the rainbow so the cloud can be seen on front and back. the fold should be on the outer edge of the rainbow,
Stitch in place to the rainbow but leave base open to stuff very lightly before closing.
This adds dimension.

Rainbow Hanger

Raindrops (make 3)

Cast on 2 sts in blue
incl into each sts - 4sts
P1 row
Incl into each - 8sts
Stst 2 rows
(P2tog) to end
B&T

To Make up

Sew from B+T end, up side seams , inserting bead as you close it up to cast
on edge. Sew closed and use invisible thread or fishing line to attach to
cloud and rainbow.
Use the same thread to make a hanging cord for the rainbow and hang up.

38

Mini Unicorn keyring

For This Project - You need.

Knitting yarns.

Dk wool in white
Dk wool in multicolour

Additional materials.

Oddments of felt in yellow
2 black seed beads - optional for eyes
Black embroider thread for nostrils and eyes if not using seed beads
One keyring, any style.
Pink sharpie for cheeks

Tools.

Size 12 needles (UK sized)
Wool needle.
Sewing needle.
Scissors.

Mini Unicorn keyring

The body and head. (One piece)

To begin, cast on 20 sts
St st 10 rows starting with K
Row 11 -(K2 tog) to end ....10 stitches
Row 12- Pwise increase into every stitch....20 sts
st st 8 rows
Row 21-(K2 tog) to end
Row 22 – (P2tog) to end
B+T

Ears

To make the ear make a finger knitted chain stitch 6 sts long, and fold over.
Stitch together to make a small triangle and attach to head each side.

Muzzle

Cast on 10 sts
start with K row
St-st 3 rows
Row 4- (p2 tog) to end
Row 5- k2tog, k1, k2tog
B+T

Base

Cast on 20 sts
K1 row
(K3, K2tog) repeat to end
(K2tog) to end
(K2tog) to end
B+T

Mini Unicorn keyring

Mane

Using your multicolored wool
Finger Knit a chain measuring 25cm

Tail

Using your multicolored wool
Finger Knit a chain measuring 15cm

To Make up Unicorn

Sew up from cast on edge to top of head and stuff. Leaving base open.
To make the neck more prominent draw wool round the neck indent
and pull tight, stitch wool into the body to secure.
The base laid flat should make a circle, sew edge seams together to
complete the circle sew to base opening to close.
The decoration of the horse /unicorn is simple.
Embroider eyes and nose in place as pictured.
Use marker to blush cheeks
The main is sewn to the forehead and looped and stitched in place,
working down center back of the head.
Do the same for the tail, making longer loops.
To attach key ring use hair colour wool to sew to top of the head,
looping stitches through several times to secure.

The Horn

On yellow felt draw a 3cm circle.
Cut out and half the circle, you only need one half for the horn.
Rill from one end to the other creating a tight cone.
Sew to the unicorns head with matching sewing thread or white.

Mini Cutesy Unicorn.

For This Project - You need.

Knitting yarns.

50 gram of White
25 gram of multicolored or colour of your choice.
Small amount of metallic gold

Additional materials.

Small amounts of craft felt in Pink
Embroidery thread in Black
Toy Stuffing – Small bag.

Tools.

No.12 needles. UK sized
Wool needle. UK sized
Sewing needle.
Scissors.

Mini Cutesy Unicorn.

Front legs, neck and head. (One piece)

Cast on 14 Sts on No.12 needles in White.
St st 2 rows.
Next row - ** K2tog, K to last 2 Sts, K2tog.
P1 row*.
Repeat from ** to * until you have 10 Sts, ending with the P row.
St st 16 rows.
Put this aside on a needle and make a second leg in the exact same way.
Once you have both legs done, put on one needle.
Put both sets of stitches on one needle with right side facing, then knit across both legs to join.
St st 10 rows.
Next row -***P2tog, P to last 2 sts , P2tog.
K1 row**.
Repeat from *** to ** until 14 Sts remain

Increase for the head as follows.
P1, (Inc 1, P1), P1
K1 row. (20 Sts)
Repeat last 2 rows once more. (30Sts)
St st 15 rows.
Next row - (K3, K2tog) to end.
Next row - (P2, P2tog) to end.
Next row - (K1, K2tog) to end.
P2 tog to end.
B+T tightly.

To make up

Sew from top of the head, down to where the neck is and stuff. Draw a little wool through the increase for head row and pull tight for neck (using an in and out stitch around the neck and pulling a little tighter to draw in).
Sew down body and stuff as you go to the point where legs begin.
Sew legs from joint between legs down each and stuff leaving bases of the feet open. There will be a flat line down back of horses head this is normal and is where the mane will be sewn on.
Leave this piece aside for now.

43

Back legs and rump.

Leg (Make 2)

Cast on 14 Sts on No.12 needles in White.
St st 2 rows.
Next row -**K2tog, K to last 2sts , K2tog
Next row - P1 row*
Repeat from ** to *, until you have 10 Sts ending with the P row
St st 16 rows
Leave on a spare needle and make 2nd leg in same way

Once second piece is knitted put both sets of stitches on one needle (20 sts)
wrong side facing and Purl across both legs
Next row - St st 11 rows
Next row - (P3, P2tog) to end
Next row - (K1, K2tog) to end
Next row - (P2tog) to end, P1
B+t tightly

To make up

Draw thread tightly and sew down to where legs meet, stuff well.
Join legs and sew down each one, stuffing and leaving bases open.

Foot base (Make 4)

Cast on 15 Sts on No.12 needles in White.
K1 row.
(K2, K2tog) to last 3 Sts - K3.
(K1, K2 tog) to end..
(K2 tog) to end.
B+T tightly.

Mini Cutesy Unicorn.

Flatten out and sew edges to make a flat circle. Sew this onto horses legs at the base, closing the base up and giving it a flat pad to stand on. Do this with all 4 legs.

Middle section of body

Cast on 10 Sts on No.12 needles in White.
St st until work measures 7.5 cm. Approx 32 rows.
Cast off.

To make up

Sew cast off edge to cast on edge, making a tube shape. Stuff lightly to hold shape and sew back legs to one open end and front legs to other - making sure the seams are facing into the tube on both pieces, and the stomach seam faces down. Add more stuffing before closing completely, to stiffen. This is quite tricky to sew together and you may find using safety pins to hold in place while sewing helpful.

Ears (make 2)

Cast on 10 Sts on No.12 needles in White.
K1 row.
Next row - P4, P2tog, P4.
Next row - K3, K2tog, K4.
Next row - (P2, P2tog) twice.
Next row - (K1, K2tog) twice.
Next row - (P2 tog) to end.
B+T tightly.

Mini Cutesy Unicorn.

Fold in half and flatten to make a triangle shape. Sew up seam, leaving it to one side of the ear and sew onto horses head at each side. Position is optional. Sew in place with seam pointing the center of head.

Muzzle

Cast on 15 Sts on No.12 needles in White.
K 1 row.
P2tog, P to last 2 sts, P2 tog.
K 1 row.
Repeat these last 2 rows until 9 Sts remain, ending on K row.
P2tog to end, P1
B+T tightly.

To make up

Draw tightly to close the end, sew up side seam. Stuff lightly and sew onto front of Unicorns face. Leave enough space on the upper part of face for eyes and fringe.

Hair

With No.12 needles and chosen hair colour
Cast on 8 Sts.
Cast off, leaving 1 st remaining on needle, use this stitch to cast on another 8 Sts.
Cast off again, leaving one St remaining on needle.
You will notice this makes the hair strands, yet keeps them joined in a line.
Continue using 20 Sts instead of 8, until you have the 2 short strands and 10 longer ones. Cast off the last one completely.

To make up.

You should have a long chain of strands which can be flattened out.
The shorter strands are the fringe and get sewn between the ears and onto the forehead. Sew remainder down the back of the head along the visible seam in a line until the shoulder area.

Mini Cutesy Unicorn.

Tail

The tail is made in exactly the same way, except casting on 25 Sts and continuing for 5 strands before casting off. It is then sewn with all the strands pulled together at top to form a tail and sewn on the rump.

Horn

With No.12 needles, double up your metallic gold wool to work as thicker wool. This gives the horn stiffness.
Cast on 6 Sts
K1 row.
P1 row.
K2tog, to end.
P1 row.
B+T tightly.

To make up

Sew up to cast on edge, stuff and sew onto unicorns face, just below fringe and centered.

To finish.

Using pink felt, cut 2 small circles and sew onto face as pictured.

Use Black embroidery thread to stitch eye detail.

Then you're done.

Pastel Una Doll

For This Project - You need.

Knitting yarns.

Chosen flesh colour 50g
Cream 50g
Pink, orange, lemon, green, blue, lilac in 50g balls
Mint green in 50g

Additional materials.

2 x 4mm toy eyes
6 micro buttons - 4 lilac, 2 green
Sharpie to blush cheeks in pale pink
Toy Stuffing – Small bag.
Micro button for the bag

Tools.

No.10 needles UK sized (3.25mm)
Wool needle.
Sewing needle.
Scissors.

Pastel Una Doll

Head and Body

Legs (make 2)

On No.10 needles and in yellow cast on 10sts
Inc Kwise into every St - 20sts
P 1 row
Inc Kwise into every St - 40sts
P 1 row
Start with K row
St St 6 rows
(K2tog) to end - 20sts
P 1 row
K1, (K3tog) 4 times, K7 - 12sts
P1 row
Add cream
St st 28 rows
Put on a spare needle to make the second leg.

Bring back two legs to one needle, with right side facing you and in Cream
K across both sets of stitches to join them - 24 sts.

The Body

Starting with P row
Join lilac
St St 23 rows in the follow
2 rows of each lilac, Blue, Green, Yellow, Orange, Pink, then repeat.
You should have pink on the needles when done
(K2tog) to end
Join flesh
P 1 row

Pastel Una Doll

Kwise Inc 1 into every st for head - 24 sts
P 1 row
(K1, Inc1) to end
St St 13 rows
(K2tog) to end
(P2tog) to end
B+T

To Make Up

Start at head, and sew down to where the legs join on. Stuff head and body and close between legs.
Sew down each leg, stuffing as you go and end at the feet, sewing foot closed in a straight line from toe to heel on the base.
Draw a length of wool around neck using an in out stitch and draw tight to define neck.

Arms (make 2)

With orange cast on 5 sts
KW Inc1 into every st - 10sts
Stst 7 rows starting with P
Join yellow
K 3 rows
Join flesh
Starting P Stst 11 rows
(K1, Inc1) to end
Stst 4 rows
(P2tog) to last st, P1
(K2tog) to end
B + T

To Make Up

Sew from hands to open cast on edge, stuff and sew the arms closed by flattening the top so the seam lies at the center back, Sew across top of arm in a straight line and leave aside for sleeve frills.

50

Skirt

Top Layer
In Cream and size 10 needles
Cast on 75sts
St st 2 rows (starting K)
K1, (Yfwd, K2tog) to end (pico edge)
P 1 row
St St 12 rows
K1 (K1, K2tog) to end
P 1 row
(K2, K2tog) to end - 28sts
P 1 row
Cast off

Under Skirt
Cast on 50sts in lilac
P 1 row
K1, (yfwd, K2 tog) to last st, K1
St st 3 rows
Join blue
Work 2 rows, then 2 rows in the following of each colour
Green, yellow, orange, pink
Working in pink from here on
Stst another 2 rows of pink
(K2tog) to end
P 1 row
Cast off

To Make up
Join the skirt pieces at the edge seams and sew them up one by one to create 2 skirts. Fold up the lower edges to create the picot edge and sew on the inside of the skirt to hold in place.
On the doll locate the middle of the torso (we used the top of the orange row) and mark for the cream skirt. Sew in place.
Below this you want to sew on the under layer leaving a small gap so the skirt sits flatter. (we sewed the under skirt to the top of the yellow row)

Sleeve Frill (Make 2)

With No.10 needles and lemon
Cast on 24sts
P 1 row
(K2tog) to end
Cast off Pwise
This is slid around the sleeve where the lemon edge is, butted against the
knit line, sewn in place, joining seam at back.
You can now sew the arms to the body as pictured.

Dungaree straps (Make 2)

In cream
Cast on 35sts
Cast off

Sew these strips to centre back of skirt and lay over shoulder, bringing to
front as pictured and secure leaving a small piece hanging over the skirt.
Sew the green micro buttons here to mimic dungaree straps.

Shoe straps

In lemon cast on 8sts
Cast off.

These are sewn across the front of each show and a micro button in lilac is
used to detail them as pictured.

Neck collar

In pink Cast on 20 sts
Cast off

Once your dungaree straps are in place this lays over them and around the
neck to create a collar. The seam is joined at the back and sewn in place to
secure.

Pastel Una Doll

Boot ankle trim (make 2)

In lemon and No 10 needles
Cast on 14sts
Cast off
Join at center back of ankle and stitch in place just above boot to tidy that
area

Bow for back of dress.

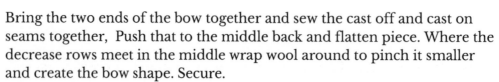

In pink cast on 5 sts
Kw incl into every st - 10sts
Stst 16 rows
(P2tog) to end - 5sts
Kw incl into every st - 10 sts
St st 16 rows
(P2tog) to end - 5 sts
Cast off

Bow centre

In pink cast on 10 sts
Cast off

Bring the two ends of the bow together and sew the cast off and cast on
seams together, Push that to the middle back and flatten piece. Where the
decrease rows meet in the middle wrap wool around to pinch it smaller
and create the bow shape. Secure.
The strip wraps around this centre piece and sewn at the back to secure.
The bow is sewn to back of the dress where dungaree straps meet.

Pastel Una Doll

The Hair

The hair is made in strips.

You will need 4 strips as follows
Cast on 15 sts in mint
Cast off leaving one stitch on the needle.
Use this to cast on another 14 more sts.
Cast off again leaving one stitch on the needle.
Repeats until you have 11 hair strands all joined together in this way. Cast off completely.

Make a row with the same number of stitches but with 5 strands.
And then make another with just 3 strands.

The hair is sewn around the head as pictured. The long rows start just about ear level and you will space them above one another until you have the crown left.
The 5 strand is folded so they fit into the gap and create a seam or hair part along the top as pictured.
The 3 strand is sewn where a fringe would lie to fill in the hair line and sit around the horn.

Be mindful of leaving gaps for the ears as you apply the hair.

Pastel Una Doll

The ears (make 2)

In cream, cast on 10sts
K1 row.
Next row - P4, P2tog, P4.
Next row - K3, K2tog, K4.
Next row - (P2, P2tog) twice.
Next row - (K1, K2tog) twice.
Next row - (P2 tog) to end.
B+T tightly.

To make up

Fold in half and flatten to make a triangle shape. Sew up seam, leaving it to one side of the ear and sew onto horses head at each side. Position is optional. Sew in place with seam pointing the center of head.

Horn

With No.10 needles, and lemon (leave a decent length tail of wool)
Cast on 6 Sts
K1 row.
P1 row.
K2tog, to end.
P1 row.
B+T tightly.

To make up

Sew up to cast on edge, stuff with the remaining tail of lemon wool and sew onto dolls upper face, just below fringe and centered.

The Face

I used flesh wool to over stitch a little nose in the centre of the face and toy eyes places as pictured.

You can use a pale pink sharpie marker to blush the cheeks.

And you're done!!   55

Lenny the Unicorn.

For This Project - You need.

The bag and scarf is not included in this pattern.

Knitting yarns.

DK wool in white, I used a 50g ball
DK wool in assorted colours or a rainbow mix ball. Small oddments.

Additional materials.

Oddments of felt in pinks and yellow
Black seed beads for eyes and nostrils, although black felt will do
Sewing threads to match your felt, or just white

Tools.

I use size 14 knitting needles or toy makers needles for a tight stitch. You can use size 12 (UK sized) if you have none
Wool needle.
Sewing needle.
Scissors.

Lenny the Unicorn.

The body and head. (One piece)

Cast on 30sts in white
Stocking stitch 20 rows
Knit 2 stitches together, repeat until end, leaving 15 stitches
Increase in every stitch to recreate 30 stitches.
This will make the Unicorns neck.
Stocking stitch 18 rows
Knit 2 stitches tog, repeat until the end (15sts)
Pearl 2 stitches together, repeat until the end. (8sts)
Cut a long length of the wool and thread through remaining stitches, pull
off needle and pull tight.
This forms the top of the head.

To make up

Stitch seams together to the base, stuff from the open bottom. Once full
run a piece of wool around the neck line and pull tightly, sewing in the
ends.

The muzzle

Cast on 20sts in white.
Sts 5 rows
K4, K2 together, K4, K2 together, K3 (13 sts)
P1 row
K3, K2 together, K3, K2 together, K3 (11 sts)
P2 together to end. (6 sts)
Break wool and thread through remaining stitches, draw up and pull titght
to close end.
Sew from this point down joining your two outer edges to create a muzzle.
Sew to face once stuffed. As pictured.

Lenny the Unicorn.

The base

This is the circular closure which completes the base of the body
Cast on 30stitches in white
Knit one row
Pearl 2 stitches together until the end (15 stitches)
Knit one row
Pearl 2 stitches together until the end (8 stitches)
Knit one row
Pearl 2 stitches together until the end (4 stitches)
Cut wool and thread through remaining stitches, pull tight.

This makes up the centre of the circle, sew edge seams together to create a flat circle, sew to base of Unicorn.

Lenny the Unicorn.

Ears (make two)

Cast on 10 stitches
Stocking stitch 3 rows
Pearl 2 together until end (5 sts)
Knit 1 row
Pearl 2 tog until end (3 sts)

Break off wool and thread through remaining stitches and pull tight.
Sew up seams to create a cone shape.
Flatten out and sew to head as pictured.

For horn

Roll a piece of triangular felt until its desired thickness, sew in place,
Tummy is an oval pink felt piece. Cheeks are pale pink circles.
Eyes and Nostrils are seed beads sewn in place as pictured.

59

Lenny the Unicorn.

Arms and Legs

Using 6 long strands folded in half , secure with length of wool creating the top of the plait, plait a 10cm long arm, tie a knot at the base to secure and trim off leaving small strands, make 2

Using 12 long strands folded in half, secure with length of wool creating the top of the plait, plait a 12cm long leg. Tie a knot at the base to secure and trim. Make two.

Sew to the body as pictured using white wool you secured at the tops of the plaits

To make hoofs

Cut rectangle strips of felt, roll around the base of the arms and legs and sew in place, cut small circles to sew on the bottoms to create the hoof look.

The rainbow hair.

Cast on 20 stitches in rainbow wool or chosen colour, cast off 19 stitches. Beginning with the single stitch left cast on another 19 stitches. Cast off 19 stitches ..... This repetitive pattern creates the hair.

Make as many strands as you like, for the last 2 strands I cast on only 14 stitches to create shorter fringe strands.

60

Lenny the Unicorn.

Tail

The tail is made in exactly the same way but using 25 stitches instead.
Secure the hair and tail using matching wool.

To finish.

Using pink felt, cut 2 small circles and sew onto face as pictured.
Cut an oval of pink felt for his stomach patch and stitch in place.

Use Black embroidery thread to stitch eye detail by sewing on black seed beads and two dot nostrils with smaller sized beads.

Then you're done.

For This Project - You need.

Knitting yarns

Ball of your chosen colour. I used a multi colour pastel in DK wool.

Additional materials

small amount of stuffing
Seed beads for eyes are optional, in black.
Black sewing thread for eyes and nose detail

Tools

No.10 needles. (UK sized)
Wool needle.
Sewing needle.
Scissors.

Left Leg

Cast on 5sts
(Incl) KW into each st
(K1, Incl) to end
Stst 4 rows starting P
P5, (P2tog x3), P4
K4, (K2tog x2), K4
Stst 20 rows

Leave on a spare needle and make other leg.

Right Leg

Cast on 5sts
(Incl) KW into each st
(K1, Incl) to end
Stst 4 rows starting P
P4, (P2tog x3), P5
K4, (K2tog x2), K4
Stst 20 rows

**Put both sets on one needle with wrong side of work facing you.
 P across both legs to join**

(K1, Incl) to end (30sts)
Stst 7 rows staring P
(K5, K2tog) to last 2 sts, K2
P1 row
(K4, K2tog) to last 2 sts, K2
P1 row
(K3, K2tog) to last 2 sts, K2
P1 row
K1, (K2tog) to last st, K1
P1 row
Shape for head
Incl in every st to end - 20sts
Stst 11 rows starting P
(K2tog) to end
(P2tog) to end
B&T

To Make Up

Sew from B&T thread down head, joining and stuffing until you get to the legs. Sew down each leg one at a time stuffing and close at base of foot. To define neck, stitch in and out around neck and pull tight before fastening off.

Muzzle

Cast on 10 sts
Stst 3 rows
(K3tog) three times, K1
B& T

To Make Up

Sew from B&T to cast on edge, stuff a little and sew to face of bear.

Arms (Make 2)

Cast on 8sts
Stst 10 rows
(K1, Incl) to end - 12sts
Stst 4 rows
(P3tog) four times
B&T

To Make Up

Sew from B&T to cast on edge stuffing as you go. Gather top of arm , pull tight and sew to side of bear , just below neckline.

Ears (make 2)

Cast on 4 sts
Incl in every st - 8sts
P1 row
(K2tog) to end
(P2tog) to end
B&T

To Make Up

Over sew around edges of ear to tidy. Gather base and sew to bears head as pictured.

Bowtie

Cast on 8sts
** P1, K to last st, P1
K1, P to last st, K1 ***
Repeat from ** to *** another twice
Cast off

To Make up

 edges of bow to neaten Stitch up center middle and gather to pinch in the center of the bow. Chain st a short cord to go around middle as a fancier detail. Sew in place and attach bow on Bear.

Where to find L.T.Marshall

Website -
https://ltmarshall.blog

Romance books -
https://www.amazon.co.uk/Carrero-5-Book/dp/B07771B5CW

Knitting patterns -

Etsy - https://www.etsy.com/uk/shop/LianaMarcel
Ravelry - https://www.ravelry.com/designers/ltmarshall-2
Lovecrafts - https://www.lovecrafts.com/en-gb/user/One-Creative-Family
Amazon - https://www.amazon.co.uk/L-T-Marshall

Facebook -
Author - https://www.facebook.com/LTMarshallauthor
Crafts - https://www.facebook.com/OCFCrafts

Twitter -
https://twitter.com/LMarshallAuthor

Instagram-
https://www.instagram.com/l.t.marshall

Youtube -
youtube.com/c/OneCreativeFamily

Printed in Great Britain
by Amazon